STAR WARS™

MILLENNIUM FALCON

STAR WARS

MILLENNIUM FALCON

WRITTEN BY MICHAEL KOGGE

INCREDI
BUILDS

A Division of Insight Editions, LP
San Rafael, California

INTRODUCTION

There are legendary starships, and then there's the *Millennium Falcon*. For over nine decades, this YT-1300 freighter has sailed across the stars, doing so much more than just hauling cargo. Under captains like Lando Calrissian and Han Solo, she's been involved in notorious gambling exchanges and epic smuggling capers. She's outraced kilometer-long star cruisers and holds an unconfirmed record for the Kessel Run. She's even helped topple the Galactic Empire and played a part in winning desperate battles against the fierce First Order. Those who have had the misfortune of confronting her despise her. Would-be spacers, on the other hand, dream of flying her.

Despite the *Falcon*'s fame, she doesn't look like much and often gets confused for lesser models of her line. Her basic shape is defined by two convex saucers welded together, with a pair of mandibles and a spherical cockpit extending out from her bow. Her hull hasn't seen a complete paint job in years, leaving visible the deep scrapes and carbon scores from blaster fire and near-fatal crashes. From exterior to interior, she seems to be held together by spacer's glue, sealing foam, and pure dumb luck—and in many cases, she actually is. This appearance works to her advantage, and there are countless stories of those who mistook her for a wreck only to be left trailing in the glow of her engines.

The beauty of the *Falcon* isn't in her looks; it's in what she can do. Her owners have customized her inside and out so that scarcely an original part remains. Souped-up engines can accelerate her to speeds that rival those of snubfighters, and in hyperspace she can travel as fast as any state-of-the-art military craft. An advanced sensor suite provides her pilots with a definite edge, and she can also evade detection with jammers and signal encrypters. When it comes to combat situations, she doesn't disappoint, either. Quad turrets on both sides pound targets with a laser barrage, while concussion missiles deliver an explosive punch. Opponents bemoan how hard she is to hit and—if a lucky hit is scored—how much harder she is to damage. Deflector shields and a durasteel hull block all but the heaviest of attacks. The *Millennium Falcon* has taken her licks over and over again and has somehow survived to fly another parsec.

MILLENNIUM FALCON

Though the *Millennium Falcon* retains the circular shape of her original YT-1300 chassis, very little of her off-the-dock instrumentation remains. Just about every system has been upgraded (or downgraded) according to the needs and desires of her owners, making the *Millennium Falcon* truly one of a kind.

TECHNICAL SPECIFICATIONS

MANUFACTURER: Corellian Engineering Corporation

MODEL: Modified YT-1300f light freighter, serial number YT 492727ZED

CLASS: Freighter

WIDTH/HEIGHT/DEPTH: 25.61 m x 34.37 m x 8.27 m

WEAPONRY: Two quad laser cannons, two concussion missile tubes, retractable blaster cannon

SHIELDS: Yes

MAXIMUM SPEED: 3,000 G (space) / 1,050 kph (atmosphere)

HYPERDRIVE: Class 0.5; backup unit Class 10

ARAKYD ST2 CONCUSSION MISSILE TUBES (2): Each launcher carries a four-missile magazine.

CEC AG-2G QUAD LASER CANNON (2): Enhanced laser actuators and gas feeds give dorsal and ventral-mounted cannons maximum range and damage.

ISU-SIM SSP05 HYPERDRIVE: Class 1 generator jury-rigged "Vandangante style" to Class 0.5

GIRODYNE SRB42 SUBLIGHT ENGINES: Major modifications include a SLAM overdrive that reroutes energy for acceleration bursts.

GELIEG 20M-CP STROBE/C-BEAM LAMPS:
Floods illumination outside the ship

LIFE SUPPORT SYSTEMS: Yes

CREW: 2 (minimum)

PASSENGERS: 6

CARGO CAPACITY: 100 metric tons

CONSUMABLES: Two months' supply

COST: Privately owned, not presently available for sale

DEFLECTOR SHIELD PROJECTORS (2):
Torplex and Nordoxicon units protect the bow from both lasers and concussion missiles while a Kuat Drive Yard generator shields the stern.

COCKPIT: Outrigger-style with transparisteel windows

HULL: Duralloy plates from an Imperial cruiser afford the *Falcon* capital ship–class armor.

FORWARD MANDIBLES:
Can latch onto docks for easy freight loading

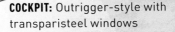

SENSOR DISH: Rectangular rectifying antenna; replaces a round military-grade model.

ESCAPE PODS (5): Padded confines built for a single passenger

GOT IT WHERE IT COUNTS

The *Falcon* can sometimes seem as temperamental as her owners. Programming her primary computer can often be as difficult as dealing with a snippy astromech droid that's never had a memory wipe. Perhaps this is her greatest asset: The *Millennium Falcon* is a ship with attitude.

COCKPIT

The cockpit houses the flight controls that command the *Falcon* through her motions. When a skilled pilot sits at the helm, magic can happen.

FORWARD CONTROLS

1 ARTICULATED YOKES (2): Oiled and loosened to steer the *Falcon* with ultra-precision. Buttons activate internal comm systems.

2 DISPLAY MONITOR: Shows general data readouts for a variety of systems, from communications and navigation to combat and sensor scans.

3 ENGINE LEVERS (2): Start the *Falcon's* sublights.

4 SENSORS: Swapped out for a suite designed for military scout ships and able to do full spectrum analysis for long-range detection.

5 THROTTLE: Adjusts fuel flow to engines.

6 VELOCITY INDICATOR: Measures current speed and direction.

7 VIEWPORT: Transparisteel panels allow side and forward visibility.

8 HYPERDRIVE LEVER: Completes circuit to send the *Falcon* into or out of lightspeed.

9 SPEED BRAKE: Can shut off the sublights and stop the *Falcon* cold.

10 AUTOPILOT SWITCH: Permits the *Falcon* to fly on her own. Also can be activated via remote.

11 WARNING LIGHT: Blinks whenever there's an emergency. Han and Chewbacca often covered it with bonding tape to minimize distraction.

12 LANDING GEAR: Deploys repulsor jets and electromagnetic grippers for locking to landing pads.

13 DEFLECTOR SHIELD CONTROLS AND DISPLAY: Operates the bow and stern units. Energy umbrella often fluctuates because the two generators are from a different manufacturer.

14 SUBSPACE RADIO: Includes standard unit with a limited range and a Chedak Frequency Agile transceiver that sends and receives intership communications within a forty-light-year radius. Rigged with a Carbanti Whistler module for encrypted messages.

HIT IT!

Giving the bulkhead a hard smack usually revives the loose connections of the instrumentation panels.

BULKHEAD

1 NAVIGATIONAL COMPUTER AND DISPLAY: Microaxial Rubicon HyD "Astrogator" uses sensor data and star charts to compute realspace trajectories and vectors for safe lightspeed travel. A backup unit has also been installed as a precaution.

2 INDICATION READOUTS FOR HYPERDRIVE, SUBLIGHT ENGINES, AND POWER SYSTEMS: Monitors health of component systems.

3 HATCH: Sized for the height of average Corellians. Taller beings have to duck to prevent bumping their craniums.

4 HATCH CONTROL SWITCH: Opens and closes the cockpit door.

5 FUEL MANAGEMENT CONSOLE: Displays intake efficiency for fine-tuning.

6 ENVIRONMENTAL CONTROLS (ALL): Adjust basic life support, air supply, and cabin pressure.

SEATING ARRANGEMENT

7 SWIVEL-MOUNTED CHAIRS (4): Two in front for pilot and copilot; two behind for passengers. The front seats have controls for comfort, and all possess safety belts and crash-webbing hooks.

A BIRD OF PREY

The *Millennium Falcon* is primed for speed, so, in most confrontations, her pilots often choose to flee. But, when necessary, the *Falcon* can put up a vicious fight that leaves her opponents wishing they'd never attacked at all.

NOT YOUR AVERAGE YT

Most commercial YT-1300 freighters possess light armaments to defend against pirates. The *Millennium Falcon* is a vessel of another stripe entirely. She's equipped with an arsenal that has broken all her manufacturers' warranties and puts many assault ships to shame.

VIEWPORT: Transparisteel windows present a clear, non-digitized view of field of battle.

CANNON BARRELS: High-volume gas feeders, black-market power cyclers, and augmented actuators that hold bigger-than-normal laser crystals produce a beam that can destroy a TIE fighter in one hit.

GUN TURRETS

The *Falcon* hosts two gun turrets: one factory-issued dorsal and a CEC AG-2G quad cannon underneath the *Falcon* in place of the standard twin. The gunnery ring can rotate, allowing reconfiguration of the cannon's positioning. Some of the more common placements of the dorsal cannon include suspension from the top of the gunwale window or springing out from the bottom.

GUNNERY SEAT: Ball-mount base swivels the seat in all directions to aid aim.

LADDER: Provides access to turrets. Missing a few rungs.

TWIN FIRING GRIPS: Triggers respond to pressure and speed of activation

AG-2G ADVANCED TACTICAL TARGETING COMPUTER: Offsets gunner delay by predicting microsecond movements of enemy craft. Can lock onto a four-meter or larger target if it remains in range for one and a half seconds.

DIRECTIONAL CONTROLS: Hand sticks raise or lower the turret. Foot pedals shift it to either side.

BUZZ OFF

Sometimes liftoffs aren't as gentle as planned, and pilots are forced to initiate the launch sequence while trying to ward off intruders who want to get onboard. Han Solo's solution was to wire a BlasTech Ax-108 surface defense blaster cannon into a compartment in the freighter's underbelly and set it to automatic targeting. While the quad lasers are designed for space combat, this "ground buzzer" is fashioned to blast away human-sized intruders—and saved Han and Chewie from unwanted visitors many, many times.

INTERIOR

Newcomers to the *Millennium Falcon* can be tempted to roam her nooks and crannies. Passengers are warned, however, not to touch open paneling. Many cables lack safety jackets.

MAIN CORRIDOR

The main corridor circles the rooms and cargo holds of the *Falcon*. Medpacs, breath masks, and fire extinguishers are stored in often-mislabeled compartments around the ship.

SECRET COMPARTMENTS: Under the deck plates of the corridor floors lie locked and alloy-plated spaces where illegal cargo—or even passengers—can be stowed in the event of an unwelcome boarding.

DOCKING RINGS: Each side of the *Falcon* has a sealed airlock for docking with space stations or other ships. The starboard hatch sees the most frequent use and features a boarding ramp for ground entry.

MAIN HOLD/LOUNGE

The central area of the ship was originally designed for cargo storage due to its proximity to the freight-loading room but is often converted by YT-1300 captains into a passenger lounge. Somewhere down the line of ownership this conversion was made to the *Falcon* and has been kept by her succession of owners, from Lando Calrissian to Han Solo to Unkar Plutt.

MAINTENANCE ACCESS: Removable floor panels lead down to a crawlway for fixing fuel and gas lines.

HOLOGAME TABLE: Chewbacca often vented his frustrations by playing the ancient game of dejarik, which kept him from yanking cables out of the ship's walls.

COMBAT REMOTE: Solo passed the time during long hyperspace journeys undertaking target practice with an Industrial Automaton Marksman-H repulsor-driven combat remote.

CREW QUARTERS

- **BUNKS:** Functional sleeping pallets, one outfitted with an Athakam II Med Unit to diagnose and treat illness and injury.

- **SONIC SHOWER:** Uses sound vibrations to scrub bipedal bodies and hair free of dirt and grime.

- **STORAGE LOCKERS:** For stashing personal effects. Locking codes have been lost for some time.

- **CLOSET:** Stores clothes and spacesuits on a hanging rack.

- **REFRESHER:** Compacts passenger waste and shoots it out a tiny airlock.

PREVIOUS OWNERS

Since the *Millennium Falcon*'s manufacture, many have sat in her cockpit. Some, like Han Solo, have warmed the seat for decades; others, only a few days or even hours.

LANDO CALRISSIAN

As a young gambler seeking his fortune, Calrissian toured the galaxy in the *Falcon*, modifying the freighter to suit his purposes and causing scandals wherever he went. But then the overconfident gambler made a most foolhardy bet and lost the vessel in a game of sabacc.

HAN SOLO

A scoundrel by the name of Han Solo was the winner of that legendary sabacc game with Calrissian, and his prize was worth more to him than any pot of credits. With his first mate Chewbacca, Solo used the vessel to transport cargo (usually of the illicit kind) throughout the galaxy. No matter how safe these smuggling runs seemed at first, the duo routinely found themselves in serious trouble. So he and Chewbacca installed all the military-grade equipment they could acquire, from deflector shields and armor plating to a 0.5 hyperdrive. They tuned the sublight engines to exceed their safety limits, allowing Solo to accomplish stunts that not even daredevil pilots would attempt. Few would disagree that it was Captain Solo who cemented the legend of the *Falcon* forever.

CHEWBACCA

Chewbacca may not have his name on the *Falcon*'s official registration—if such a thing exists—but there is no doubt that the freighter is as much his as she was Han Solo's, despite what the Wookiee's counterpart said in public. Chewie has made minor tweaks to the ship to fit his size and major adjustments that keep the *Falcon* running in even the most precarious of situations. No one has had a better rapport with the freighter's internal systems than Chewbacca, although the *Falcon* can test the limits of the Wookiee's engineering skill, as well as his patience.

UNKAR PLUTT

How exactly the *Falcon* came to be just another derelict on Jakku remains a tale best told in backwater cantinas. Suffice it to say, the ship passed from Solo to Ducain to a group called the Irving Boys before becoming one of scrap-dealer Unkar Plutt's garbage hulks. Plutt added a compressor and fuel pump in an effort to get the freighter off the ground. Despite Plutt's modifications, the *Falcon* remained grounded for years in Niima Outpost until someone with the right touch woke her from her dormancy.

REY

Nineteen-year-old Rey brought life back to the *Falcon*'s engines and launched the ship once again into the stars. Rey had logged thousands of hours flying YT-1300s on her simulator—and the *Falcon*'s peculiarities posed no problem for someone who regularly modified her own speeder. When Solo and Chewbacca found the *Falcon* again, Rey's piloting skills so impressed Solo that instead of dumping her off at the nearest inhabited planet, he asked her to join his crew.

FAMOUS FLIGHTS

The flight logs of the *Millennium Falcon* prove that pilot-training holos should be taken with a grain of spice. Just about everything deemed impossible in spaceflight has been done by the *Falcon* with an ostentatious flair that flouts the basic physics of the universe—except, that is, when her systems fail!

KESSEL RUN

Less than twelve parsecs—that's the Kessel Run record Han Solo claims he made in the *Falcon*, though incredulity among spacers pushed the number to fourteen. Even at that speed, this ranks the *Falcon* as the fastest ship ever to transport illegal spice from the mines of Kessel along its hazardous and highly guarded hyperspace route.

ESCAPE VECTORS

The Death Star's tractor beam dragged the *Millennium Falcon* into its main hangar but couldn't keep her there. Obi-Wan Kenobi, the Jedi Master who had commissioned the freighter for travel, managed to power off the beam, giving his fellow passengers a chance to break free of the battle station. With Han Solo and Luke Skywalker in the gun turrets and Chewbacca at the controls, the *Falcon* thwarted TIE fighter sentries to flee into hyperspace.

NICK OF TIME

While the rebel pilots lifted off in their starfighters to do battle with the Death Star, Han Solo refused to join their cause. He loaded the *Falcon* with credits to pay off the crime lord Jabba the Hutt. Nevertheless, goaded by angry barks from his first mate, Solo changed the *Falcon*'s course and flew straight into the war zone. His triggering of the *Falcon*'s cannons sent Darth Vader's TIE spinning off into space, giving Luke Skywalker the opportunity he needed to fire the proton torpedoes that destroyed the first Death Star.

TUMMY TROUBLES

Unable to jump to lightspeed and escape the Imperial Starfleet, Han Solo braved preposterous odds and took the *Falcon* into the dense Anoat asteroid belt. He and Chewbacca orchestrated a ballet of maneuvers through the spinning field of rocks, avoiding lethal impacts by the slimmest of margins. Many of the chasing TIE fighters, however, weren't so lucky. The thinning of their numbers gave the *Falcon* the chance to duck into a chasm on a large asteroid and evade the remaining TIEs. What the *Falcon* and her crew soon discovered was that the cave they landed inside wasn't a cave at all, but the gullet of a hungry space slug!

SNOWBLASTIN'

Darth Vader and a cadre of Imperial snowtroopers busted into the hangar of the rebel base on Hoth to discover the *Millennium Falcon* was still grounded. Pummeled by their blasters, the *Falcon* fired back with her ground cannon and managed to launch from the frozen planet with cold engines and a malfunctioning hyperdrive.

FLOTSAM AND JETSAM

The *Millennium Falcon* always looked to be on the verge of a breakdown, and truthfully, she was. This helped when Han Solo had her drift away with the refuse left by the Imperial Starfleet. The Empire's gunners couldn't tell that the *Falcon* was more than a big piece of trash! Unfortunately, the bounty hunter Boba Fett was canny enough to see through the ruse and followed the ship to Bespin's Cloud City.

BESPIN BREAKAWAY

While having her hyperdrive repaired in Cloud City, the *Millennium Falcon* lost her captain, Han Solo, when he was captured by Boba Fett. Fortunately, she regained her former owner, Lando Calrissian. The gambler-turned-baron administrator was not quite the hotshot pilot that Solo was, yet was still adept at flying the *Falcon*, especially when paired with Chewbacca. The two of them skirted the *Falcon* around TIE sentries to retrieve an injured Luke Skywalker from a weathervane, then darted off to safety, evading Imperial capture.

RESCUE RANGER

The *Millennium Falcon* became the mobile head-quarters for Calrissian, Princess Leia Organa, and Chewbacca during their plan to rescue Han Solo from the vile gangster Jabba the Hutt. Calrissian took up employment as a skiff guard in Jabba's palace, gaining the crime lord's trust. Princess Leia and Chewbacca landed the *Falcon* in the Tatooine desert near the palace, then carried out the operation to save Han.

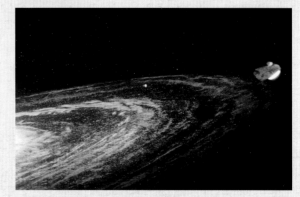

DEATH STAR DESTROYER

When Han Solo and Chewbacca decided to join the Rebellion's commandos on a ground mission to Endor, Lando Calrissian once again helmed the *Falcon*, with the Sullustan Nien Nunb as his copilot. Together they flew the *Falcon* through the girders and pipework of the semicompleted (but fully functional) second Death Star, eluding TIEs to fire a missile barrage at the reactor core. The resulting explosion brought down the Death Star and would have also consumed the *Falcon* if not for a timely acceleration boost from her engines.

JAKKU JUKES

Abandoned at Jakku's Niima Outpost airfield, the *Millennium Falcon* hadn't flown for years until a young scrap-scavenger named Rey started her engines. Rey proved a natural in the *Falcon's* chair. She wove the freighter through the innards of a crashed Star Destroyer and flipped her top-over-bottom so that Finn, a deserting stormtrooper who was manning the turret, could shoot down their TIE pursuers.

HYPERSPACE HEROICS

Han Solo once said that jumping to lightspeed wasn't like dusting crops—one wrong calculation could send a ship into a supernova. However, when he and his crew were facing certain death from monstrous rathtars and the thugs of Kanjiklub and the Guavian Death Gang, he put his trust in the *Falcon's* systems and pulled the hyperspace lever while she was parked inside the hangar of his old bulk freighter. In defiance of any sane pilot's judgment, the *Falcon* safely hit lightspeed, and its passengers escaped.

STARKILLER SLALOM

With Han Solo and Chewbacca once again at her helm, the *Millennium Falcon* risked colossal odds and achieved the impossible: She penetrated the fluctuation gaps in Starkiller Base's deflector shields while traveling at lightspeed. Nonetheless, she came out of hyperspace too fast and skimmed along the planet's snowy surface to halt right at the edge of a cliff.

FORCE *FALCON*

After the loss of his friend, Chewbacca happily honored Han Solo's offer to Rey to join the *Falcon*'s crew. Their first trip together as pilot and copilot of the *Millennium Falcon* was to travel to the lost planet where the galaxy's last Jedi Master, Luke Skywalker, resided.

BEHIND THE SCENES

"The flying hamburger was my favorite design."

– *Star Wars* creator George Lucas on the *Millennium Falcon*'s iconic shape

SKULL & CROSSBONES

For most of the production of the first film, *Star Wars: A New Hope*, released in 1977, Han Solo's freighter was referred to as the "pirate ship." The film's original designer, Colin Cantwell, fashioned the vessel into an elongated triangle that had an engine rack at its base and a windowed cockpit at its vertex.

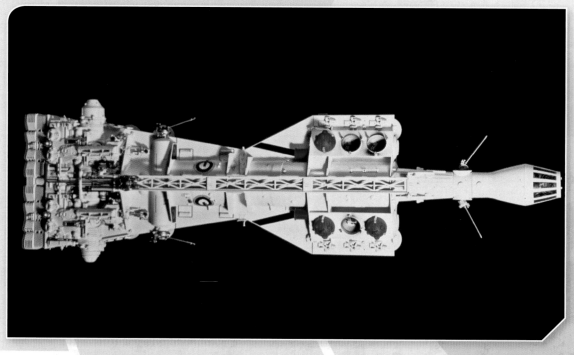

COURSE CORRECTION

George Lucas's special effects company, Industrial Light & Magic (ILM) had just finished constructing a $25,000 seven-foot-long working mod of the pirate ship based on Cantwell's prototype when Lucas decided to change the design. He felt it looked too much like a ship from the new television series *Space: 1999* and wanted something more original— more radial than triangular. On a flight from London, he conceived a hamburger-like shape that he felt would give the ship more personalit

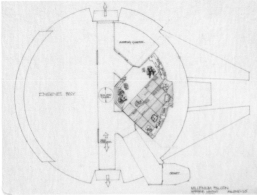

NEW WHEELS

Concept artist Joe Johnston took Lucas's notes and drew freighters with inverted saucer shapes. He streamlined the hull, added freight-loading mandibles in the front, and tricked out the engines to make it look as if Han Solo had "hot-rodded" his ship. One of those sketches became the basis for the *Falcon*.

HUNK OF JUNK

The conduits, piping, and mechanical components that detail the *Millennium Falcon*'s hull were all cannibalized pieces from off-the-shelf model kits. Sometimes ILM model makers would head to a distributor's warehouse and fill up shopping carts with $1,500 in boxed Ferrari and World War II vehicle kits.

OLD COCKPIT

To save time when constructing the second version of the *Falcon*, chief model maker Grant McCune and his team chopped off the original's spherical cockpit and attached it to the new saucer-shaped vessel that was built. The rest of the first pirate ship was repurposed as Princess Leia's blockade runner.

ABOVE Ralph McQuarrie captures the original rectilinear form of the *Millennium Falcon* in this early production painting. Princess Leia's blockade runner would later use this design, though the spherical cockpit will be kept for the *Falcon*.

BELOW Luke Skywalker and his companions get their first glimpse of Han and Chewie's "hunk of junk" in Mos Eisley's Docking Bay 94. (Production painting by Ralph McQuarrie)

ABOVE The *Millennium Falcon* races to safety after Lando Calrissian fires the ship's missiles into the second Death Star's main reactor. Wedge Antilles provides backup in his X-wing. (Production painting by Ralph McQuarrie)

BELOW *The Force Awakens* concept artist Doug Chiang showcases the Falcon's deft maneuverability as it skims the hull of a crashed Star Destroyer on Jakku.

HYPERSPACE TUNNEL

The miniature and optical unit at Industrial Light & Magic spent months generating the "jump to lightspeed" effect when Han Solo pulls the *Falcon*'s hyperspace lever in the original film. To show the *Falcon* zipping off into infinity, first cameraman Richard Edlund moved the camera toward a Polaroid of the ship while zooming out with the lens.

MONSTER MASH

Jon Berg and Phil Tippett sculpted ten small creatures out of rubber, latex, and foam to represent pieces from the holochess game that Chewbacca plays against R2-D2 aboard the *Falcon* in the original *Star Wars*. The sculptures were shot against a black velvet backdrop using painstaking stop-motion animation techniques where each creature was moved ever so slightly and photographed to create each film frame. The voices were all performed by sound designer Ben Burtt and filtered to sound tinny and alien. The chess set made a surprise return in *The Force Awakens*, lovingly re-created by Phil Tippett himself.

THE *FALCON* AND THE MUSTANG

The slowed-down sound of pistons from World War II–era P-51 Mustang bombers gave voice to the *Millennium Falcon*'s sublight engines.

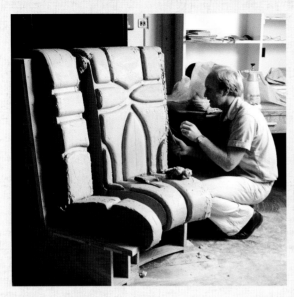

LONG ODYSSEY

Lucas instructed production designer John Barry that the *Falcon*'s interior should resemble what a spaceship from *2001: A Space Odyssey* would look like after weathering two centuries of star travel.

SPACE BALLET

Photographic and time constraints restricted how spaceships could move in the original *Star Wars* film, much to Lucas's dismay. He envisioned the vessels making dynamic, acrobatic maneuvers, so he pushed the envelope in *The Empire Strikes Back* and had the *Millennium Falcon* navigate a dense asteroid field. This required model makers to build a smaller, two-foot version of the *Falcon* to accommodate the motion-control camera. They even put together a miniature *Falcon* that could fit in the palm of one's hand and be to the correct scale when attached to the hull of an eight-foot-long Star Destroyer!

FALCON AWAKENS

The Force Awakens co-production designer Darren Gilford used the original *Millennium Falcon* blueprints to construct a near-perfect replica of the ship. Harrison Ford had one request: to add springs to the cockpit toggle switches so that they really flipped, unlike in the previous trilogy!

INTERVIEW WITH LORNE PETERSON

Lorne Peterson was one of the primary model makers for both the original and prequel *Star Wars* trilogies. He became the chief of the model shop during production of *The Empire Strikes Back* and supervised the model department when it grew to more than one hundred builders for *Revenge of the Sith*. He is also the author of *Sculpting a Galaxy*, a book published by Insight Editions that recounts his experience assembling the famous spaceships, vehicles, and miniature environments from the first six *Star Wars* films.

HOW DID YOU FIRST BECOME INVOLVED IN HOLLYWOOD MODEL-MAKING?

It was really by accident. I graduated in fine art, but all the teaching jobs were gone, so I worked in the industrial design field for several years, from the late sixties to mid-seventies. McDonald's used to have a restaurant playground called McDonaldland that featured characters like the Hamburglar. I got a job carving those characters out of big blocks of foam, and it happened that the only place we could rent a big warehouse type of space to sculpt these pieces was on a film studio lot. There I came face-to-face with a guy I knew from the design department at Long Beach State. He said to me, "There's a science fiction film we're working on, and we've had a really hard time finding model makers. Do you think you'd be interested in a two-month assignment?" Two months turned into two years, which turned into twenty years, which turned into nearly forty years.

WHAT WAS YOUR FIRST MODEL PROJECT ON *STAR WARS*?

Jonathan Erland, my partner at the small design company we owned, and I were hired to do the Death Star, which meant crawling around on your knees all day to attach thousands of windows and reflectors. The Death Star was a big thing, like four living rooms put together, and to get to the center of it, we had these big foam pads for our knees. You kind of limp after a whole day of being out on the Death Star!

HOW WAS THE *MILLENNIUM FALCON* MODEL PITCHED TO YOU?

George Lucas conceived of it traveling like a sunfish. He imagined it being flat on the ground just as you normally see it, but then as it lifted off the ground, the cockpit rotated so it could be straight up and down when it flew. But the sunfish thing died almost instantaneously. It never was flown that way. The cockpit was always in alignment with the flatness of it.

CAN YOU DESCRIBE THE PROCESS OF BUILDING THE STARSHIPS?

It turned out that we didn't need orthographic drawings. We took the shape of the ship from sketches and made a mock-up of foam core and cardboard so that everybody could look at it. We had to make some kind of estimate as to how much it would weigh and how strong the frame would have to be. For models like the *Millennium Falcon*, the X-wing, or the Star Destroyer, they all needed electrical, air cooling, and mounting systems. So you had to start almost as if you're building a car. You had to build a welded aluminum framework that had mounting points in six different spots. Then you put in a loom so that the electrical system is mounted to all six of those points. Finally, you installed a cooling system so that compressed air can be pumped in, and the halogen lights didn't melt the model.

HOW DID KIT-BASHING—USING PARTS AND PIECES FROM RETAIL MODELS—BECOME AN INTEGRAL PART IN COMPLETING THE FINAL MODEL?

Lots of the parts had to be able to come off, just like if you had to get into a car and work on the engine. Because if things went wrong with the model's cooling or electrical systems, we had to be able to take pieces off to fix the problem. We would buy duplicates at wholesale prices of kits of Formula One cars, German and Russian tanks, and Japanese models of airplanes and ships. The *Millennium Falcon*'s rear engine ports were a mix of Ferrari suspension pieces and the back end of Panzer tanks.

WHAT WERE YOUR CONTRIBUTIONS TO THE *MILLENNIUM FALCON*?

I must have shown some ability to make patterns and use kit parts and pieces, because very soon after the Death Star I was asked to work on the *Millennium Falcon*. They instructed me to do the rear-end section first, the places where the engines were. Everybody liked the work I did, and that set the tone for what was to be done on the other parts of the ship. I graduated after I did the upper rear section, where all the exhaust engines are, and progressed to doing the hallways that lead out from the edges. By that time, other people had jumped on the project. The underside isn't as distinctive as the top, since I did that all by myself. And there was never any talk about the fact my two-month period of employment was up. It just disappeared!

WHY DO YOU THINK THE *MILLENNIUM FALCON* HAS RESONATED SO DEEPLY IN POPULAR CULTURE?

When you think of some of the other ships, you don't associate a personality as much. Try to think of a personality with a Y-wing. You can't. They have pilots, but they're not Harrison Ford. If it was Joe Schmoe who drove the thing, it wouldn't be the same. And then there's everything that happened

around the *Falcon*. Most of the films' funny parts, dramatic parts, and tearful parts happened in relation to this ship. That makes it more special than some of the others—it's a character in itself. I just happened to luck out that I spent quite a bit of time building the ship and got to feel like I was the father of the *Millennium Falcon* in a way, the chief mentor.

ANY SPECIAL TIPS FOR ASPIRING MODEL MAKERS?

First of all, be very careful and wear safety glasses so that the superglue doesn't splash in your eyes—that happened to me three times where I glued my eyes shut! Also, be careful which end of the X-Acto blade you're holding. Keep the blade away from you. But most of all—have fun.

MAKE IT YOUR OWN

One of the great things about IncrediBuilds models is that each one is completely customizable. The untreat natural wood can be decorated with paints, pencils, pens—the list goes on and on!

Before you start building and decorating your model, read through the included instruction sheet so you understand how all the pieces come together. Then, choose a theme and make a plan. The *Millennium Falcon* has had many owners. How would you modify the ship if it were yours? Here are some sample projects to get those creative juices flowing.

It will be easier to cr the *Millennium Falcor* you build it. Read thro the craft instruction see the best way to d for each project.

MILLENNIUM FALCON REPLICA

When making a replica, it's always good to study an actual image of what you are trying to copy. Look closely at the images in this book and brainstorm how you can re-create them.

WHAT YOU NEED
- Red, beige, gray, white, and black paint
- Gray chalk pastel
- Cotton swab

WHAT YOU MIGHT WANT
- Piece of sandpaper
- Detail brush (18/0 size or smaller)

1. Begin assembling the model, but stop after *step 11*.
2. Paint the entire assembled piece light gray. Let dry.
3. Keep building the model until *step 17*.
4. Turn the model upside down and paint the underside and edges of the model light gray.
5. Finish assembling the model.
6. Finish your base coat by painting the bottom of the model (including the landing gear) gray.
7. Paint the top of the *Millennium Falcon* and the cockpit white.

8. After the paint is dry, start adding details. Start by painting the engraved lines gray.
9. Add the red and beige blocks of color next. Refer to the photo for placement.
10. Paint the rear heat vents black and add other small black details as you like.
11. To finish, rub chalk pastel—using a cotton swab—around the ship to add some weathering.

TIP: Use sandpaper in between coats of paint for a smoother finish.

BATTLE-DAMAGED MILLENNIUM FALCON

From the Battle of Yavin to the Battle of Endor, the *Millennium Falcon* has seen more than her fair share of firefights. Try your hand at making the iconic ship look as if it has just emerged from battle.

WHAT YOU NEED

White, black, light gray, dark gray, red (and/or orange), and beige paint
Paintbrush
Sharp pencil

WHAT YOU MIGHT WANT

Old dry paintbrush with rough bristles

TIP: Don't worry if you don't have gray paint. You can mix the white and black paint to make gray. Add more white for a lighter gray or black for a darker gray.

1. Follow steps 1 through 7 for the *Millennium Falcon* Replica, but use white paint instead of gray.
2. Trace all of the engraved lines with a sharp pencil. The pencil will leave a thin line on each side of the engraving to add some depth.
3. Add the red block details.
4. Using the beige paint, start dabbing "sand" and "dirt" onto the *Millennium Falcon*. Use your paintbrush to blend it in with background color.
5. Next, the *Millennium Falcon* needs some soot. Repeat step 4 with gray paint until you achieve your desired effect.
6. Add the black details to the cockpit, maintenance access ports, and the rear heat vents. The added swaths of black around the rear heat vents give the *Falcon* a dirty, battle-worn look.
7. Paint the fire damage.

PROTON TORPEDO DAMAGE

Paint an oval-shaped outline in red (and/or orange). Feather the outside edges to look like flames by dragging your brush softly from inside the shape to the outside.

Draw a slightly smaller oval in black. The red "flames" should still show.

Paint another smaller oval in gray. The red and black should still show.

Keep layering lighter and lighter shades of gray until you achieve the effect you desire.

LASER CANNON DAMAGE

1. Dab black paint into small spots.
2. Paint slightly smaller gray patches on top of the black spots to show where lasers may have punched through the *Falcon's* hull.

TIP: To make your paint more transparent, use an already-wet paintbrush. This will help create a lighter wash of color. But be careful—too much water and the color could bleed all over the surface.

SOURCES

Blackman, Haden. *Star Wars: The New Essential Guide to Vehicles and Vessels*. New York: Del Rey, 2003.

Bray, Adam, Cole Horton, Kerrie Dougherty, and Michael Kogge. *Star Wars: Absolutely Everything You Need to Know*. New York: Dorling Kindersley, 2015.

Bouzereau, Laurent. *Star Wars: The Annotated Screenplays*. New York: Del Rey, 1997.

Dougherty, Kerrie, Curtis Saxton, David West Reynolds, and Ryder Windham. *Star Wars Complete Vehicles*. New York: Dorling Kindersley, 2013.

Fry, Jason. *Star Wars: The Force Awakens Incredible Cross-Sections*. New York: Dorling Kindersley, 2015.

Hidalgo, Pablo. *Star Wars: The Force Awakens: The Visual Dictionary*. New York: Dorling Kindersley, 2015.

Peterson, Lorne. *Sculpting a Galaxy*. San Rafael, CA: Insight Editions, 2006.

Rinzler, J.W. *The Making of Star Wars: The Definitive Story Behind the Original Film*. New York: Del Rey, 2007.

——. *The Sounds of Star Wars*. San Francisco: Chronicle, 2010.

——. *Star Wars: The Blueprints*. Seattle: 47North, 2013.

Slavicsek, Bill and Curtis Smith. *The Star Wars Sourcebook*. Honesdale, PA: West End Games, 1987.

Smith, Bill. *Star Wars: The Essential Guide to Vehicles and Vessels*. New York: Del Rey, 1996.

Windham, Ryder. *Star Wars: Millennium Falcon Owner's Workshop Manual*. Del Rey: New York, 2011.

ABOUT THE AUTHOR

MICHAEL KOGGE's other recent work includes *Empire of the Wolf*, an epic graphic novel about werewolves in ancient Rome, and the junior novels for *Batman v Superman* and *Star Wars: The Force Awakens*, along with the *Star Wars Rebels* series of books. He resides online at www.michaelkogge.com, while his real home is located in Southern California.

IncrediBuilds™
A Division of Insight Editions LP
PO Box 3088
San Rafael, CA 94912
www.insighteditions.com

Find us on Facebook: www.facebook.com/InsightEditions
Follow us on Twitter: @insighteditions

Library of Congress Cataloging-in-Publication Data available.

ISBN: 978-1-68298-010-1

Publisher: Raoul Goff
Acquisitions Manager: Robbie Schmidt
Art Director: Chrissy Kwasnik
Designer: Edwin Kuo
Executive Editor: Vanessa Lopez
Managing Editor: Molly Glover
Senior Editor: Chris Prince
Production Editor: Elaine Ou
Associate Editor: Katie DeSandro
Production Manager: Thomas Chung
Production Assistant: Sam Taylor
Craft and Instruction Development: Rebekah Piatte
Model Design: Tony Gao, Team Green

Insight Editions, in association with Roots of Peace, will plant two trees for each tree used in the manufacturing of this book. Roots of Peace is an internationally renowned humanitarian organization dedicated to eradicating land mines worldwide and converting war-torn lands into productive farms and wildlife habitats. Roots of Peace will plant two million fruit and nut trees in Afghanistan and provide farmers there with the skills and support necessary for sustainable land use.

Manufactured in China by Insight Editions

10 9 8 7 6 5 4 3 2 1